P9-BZH-642

William E. Russell Elem Schl
Library Boston Public Schools

All About Animals

What's a REPTILE?

Anna Kaspar

PowerKiDS
press™

New York

Published in 2013 by The Rosen Publishing Group, Inc.
29 East 21st Street, New York, NY 10010

Copyright © 2013 by The Rosen Publishing Group, Inc.

All rights reserved. No part of this book may be reproduced in any form without permission in writing from the publisher, except by a reviewer.

First Edition

Editor: Amelie von Zumbusch
Book Design: Ashley Drago

Photo Credits: Cover, pp. 5, 12–13, 15, 24 (desert) Shutterstock.com; pp. 6, 24 (scales) Hemera/Thinkstock; p. 9 © www.iStockphoto.com/Christine Newman; pp. 10, 24 (hatch) © www.iStockphoto.com/Mark Kostich; pp. 16, 24 (fangs) © www.iStockphoto.com/Maria Dryfhout; pp.18–19 © www.iStockphoto.com/Bernhard Richter; p. 20 © www.iStockphoto.com/ Omar Ariff; p. 23 © www.iStockphoto.com/Christine Glade.

Library of Congress Cataloging-in-Publication Data

Kaspar, Anna.
  What's a reptile? / by Anna Kaspar. — 1st ed.
      p. cm. — (All about animals)
  Includes index.
  ISBN 978-1-4488-6134-7 (library binding) — ISBN 978-1-4488-6226-9 (pbk.) —
  ISBN 978-1-4488-6227-6 (6-pack)
  1. Reptiles—Juvenile literature. I. Title.
  QL644.2.K37 2012
  597.9—dc23
                                        2011016910

Manufactured in the United States of America

CPSIA Compliance Information: Batch #CS12PK: For Further Information contact Rosen Publishing, New York, New York at 1-800-237-9932

Contents

Crocodiles are reptiles! Turtles, lizards, snakes, and alligators are reptiles, too.

Reptiles are a kind of animal. All reptiles have **scales**.

Reptiles breathe air. Reptiles that live underwater must come up to breathe.

Most mother reptiles lay eggs.
Babies **hatch** from the eggs.

Reptiles move faster when they are warm. They lie in the sun to warm up.

Most reptiles eat other animals. Pythons sense the heat of the animals they eat!

Rattlesnakes have teeth called **fangs**. Their bite makes people sick.

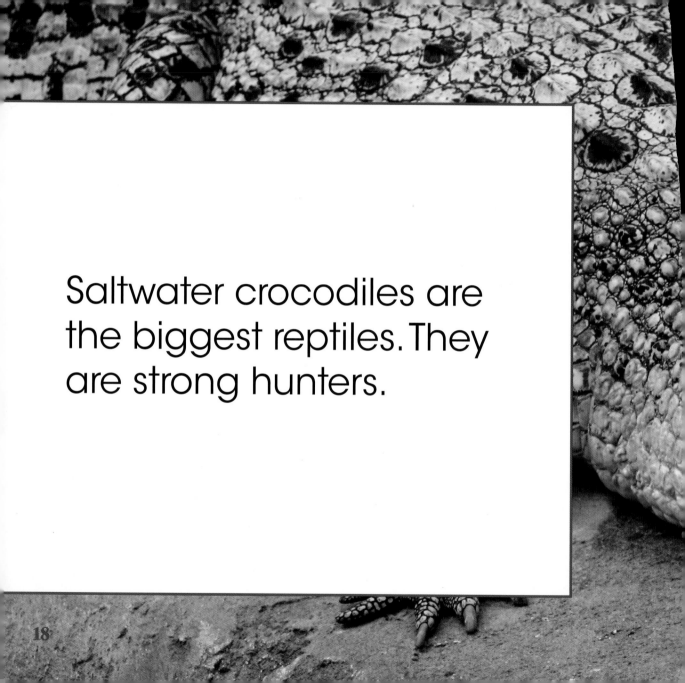

Saltwater crocodiles are the biggest reptiles. They are strong hunters.

Reptiles live in lots of places.
King cobras live in Asia.

Gila monsters live in **deserts**. Other reptiles live in forests, fields, and water.

WORDS TO KNOW

desert   fangs   hatch   scales

INDEX

WEB SITES

Due to the changing nature of Internet links, PowerKids Press has developed an online list of Web sites related to the subject of this book. This site is updated regularly. Please use this link to access the list:
www.powerkidslinks.com/aaa/reptile/

24